Bread & Bisous

DONNA GRACE

Bread & Bisous

Poems

by Donna Grace

Buffalo, New York
Copyright © 2024 by LitGarden Writers
All Rights Reserved
Printed in the United States of America

ISBN 979-8-218-39476-9

Copies of this publication may be purchased online, or directly through Donna Grace at LitGarden Writers, donna4grace@gmail.com

Front cover: Generated with AI · March 16, 2024 at 10:25 AM

Edited by George Grace

For George

Table of Contents

Acknowledgments

Special thanks to my husband and mentor, George Grace, for showing me, in his voluminous works of poetry, how to take my feelings, thoughts, and memories out to play, and for his LitGarden Writers Group that opened the floodgates to welcome all sorts of poets, ideas, interpretations, and genres. Along with George, the poems in this book were read, critiqued, and edited by the multi-talented members of LitGarden Writers: Scott Williams, Michael Delaney, Kate Willoughby, Joe Todaro, Lynn Ciesielski, Sara Ries Dziekonski, and Joe Chamberlain.

Thanks to Lynn Ciesielski, as host of Circleformance, for giving me my first reading; Sandy McPherson Carrubba Geary and Bill Geary at the Screening Room; Gunilla Kester, Rabbi Alex Lazarus-Klein, and Irene Sipos at the Buffalo Corner; Scott Williams and Stephen Lewandowski at Sea of Coffee Reading Series; Tim Joyce at Dog Ears, and ryki zuckerman at the Literary Café at Center for Inquiry for kindly offering me the featured reader spot at their poetry venues. Thanks to Sinead Tyrone for hosting an open mic poetry series at the Cabernet Café in Williamsville. I am deeply grateful to friends Melinda Schneider, Jan and Pat Feldballe, and Patricia Tansey; and special thanks to Nancy Rybczynski, Annemarie Jason, and Jana Mertz for their willingness to help fine-tune my poetry.

Hats

We used to know workers
by the hats they wore,
when one was enough—
hospital corridors
with cresting waves of nurses
in starched white caps,
and the Texaco man's
red star ablaze
on his green attendant's cap.

Now workers have to wear so many
it's not surprising to see them
collapsing under the weight
of all those hats.

I threw my hat in the ring once, and lost.
Are more people talking through their hats these days?

My cat likes to curl up in the garden hat
sitting next to me on the sofa
while he stares into my face
and dreams of shimmering swimmers
in fish tanks.

I have a friend who buys hats,
but because she doesn't wear them—
red velvet, orange silk,
green organza, and yellow linen—
they are gifts that smile at me
from the shelf in my closet.

I had a great aunt who made
so many Victorian hats
she kept them in a special bedroom
behind a closed door.
She would take away the quarter
my uncle gave me to buy a soda,
give me a sliver of dry lard soap
and send me out in my bathing suit
without a hat
to bathe in the puddle
on the busy sidewalk
in the summer rain.

Shell Shocked

You might have seen him,
a long shadow of a man.
Handsome once,
when his eyes sparkled.
Now they told a different story:

In a word:
Burma

You might have seen him,
hollowed out,
maybe looked your way
but all he saw was the next bar,
staggering to get the next drink
shoulders bent from carrying the dead
along the same road to Oblivion.

Early Days

On hot summer afternoons
Aunt Genevieve would take me
on walks along the rapids
roaring above the cliffs of Niagara
leaving us wrapped
in cool raincoats of mist.
On the rock jutting out of the churning chaos
 one seagull took center stage
to charm camera-snapping honeymooners
for future field trips
through the family photo album.

The sun coaxed
vanity from blushing dogwoods,
middle-aged by now, in tree years,
shaped by the wind
for a lifetime
shadowing rowdy waters
and wildflowers flushed
and dripping with perfume.

I would return home
to familiar voices
drifting from deadbeat houses
through treeless, mangy yards
suffocating in yellow clouds of steel
on arc-shaped, dead-end streets.

Endangered

Well beyond dazzling neon and smoky rooms
of the desert gambling towns

where twilight shadows
paint the mountains amethyst
along Tonopah Highway,

mustangs rounded the arroyo's bend,
soft manes whirling in the arid breeze
tails fanning the piney air,
clouds of labored breaths
nourishing hungry forests of shivering aspens.

My jealous heart watched
a mare tenderly
nudge her foal to join the herd,
to drink from the pond
where rushing rivulets pool,
swollen with snowmelt.

Our natural world lay dying
at the hands of presidents dismantling,
so now, when ranchers and herders
can slaughter the steeds,
who will be the stewards of soil and seeds
for desert denizens' safekeeping
and grazing for their cattle and sheep?

I live in a distant flatland now,
where dusk settles over
rooftops and church steeples,
where beauty lies
in the sun blinking through a passel of leaves
in the sky sprinkled with the brightest stars
and yards full of night under the alabaster moon.

Bearing Wounds

Our Lace Curtain and Shanty Irish
lived to tell
but rarely told of the Potato Blight, the famine walls,
how they survived coffin ships

to America with nothing
but pockets lined with hope
to set up house in a tenement
to raise another line of road pavers, ditch diggers,
quarry owners,

who lived to tell but rarely told
of the premonition and escape before the Austin flood,
wounds sliced open by the bloody suicide,
a papist haberdasher in the rural town of Barker
gone bankrupt
gone mad
after hooded agents of terror on horseback
set ablaze the parish St. Bernard,
the hamlet that night
a hell of fiery crosses.

With no one to hold your hand,
you foundered,
caught in the talons of superstitious scolds
ready to scoff and admonish,
to pass off mourning as self-indulgence.

Your sorrow frozen like the remnant
of December's snow in March,
a solitary mound of icy charcoal
along the roadside,
once warmed by the Spring sun,
you began to thaw,
weep.

Men of Steel

I no longer wonder why
I search for my father
through old photographs of steel mills
for the arrangement of machinery
feel the searing heat
oozing sweat from every pore
in the Open Hearth
that took forty years
to grind him down.
Somewhere between
blood-soaked shirts on the picket line
and last call at Curly's gin mill
he dreamed in aquamarine
of golf games at sunrise
swan dives at sunset
cradled in a hammock
on a palm tree beach
until his time would drift
to a stop.

Choices

On the bus the morning after high school graduation,
the saffron sunrise flittered across seats and aisles
as I breathed in the oaks and maples.
Downtown, homeless men slept dreamless in the
doorways
of buildings with indoor plumbing,
desks arranged in graveyard symmetry
guarded by white collar men in windowed offices.

Yesterday, it was farewell to friends
as they went off to work at summer jobs
through family connections
before heading off to college.
Today, marching to *my* father's orders,
I hit the typing pool.

After I entered the hospital
through the worker's entrance,
the boss offered a chair
in front of the picture window.
Hired.
Down, down, down, the concrete stairway,
the maximum-security steel door
clanged shut behind me
and echoed through fusty tunnels
of lights flickering fluorescent.

Inside the door
of the Medical Records Department,
women looked up, nodded,
then motioned me to the gray metal desk
wedged between a concrete slab
where I imagined a window should be,
and endless rows of metal racks bulging with folders,
where the shuffling of papers
and the tapping of typewriter keys
whittled away the soul
on a pauper's salary.

Penance

On late Sunday afternoons,
beyond the kitchen window,
the sun slashes through blue gray clouds
and glints off icicles like shards of glass.

I pluck this moment from a mélange of moments,
a sepia photograph framed and
hanging above my memory's hearth
the long walks to Mass with my father
after he pulled double shifts at the steel plant.

Waiting by the door
as he came into view, trudging through deep snow,
weighed down by the knapsack filled with work clothes
slung over his shoulder,

if given a choice, I still would have gone along.
I would not leave him to face alone yet another hostile
world.
To what did he owe the patriarchy anyway
that so despised this poor working man, and his
daughter?

Arctic winds fought with me over my hat,
pelted my cheeks,
tore at my fingers through flimsy gloves
clawed their way up my sleeves and down my back,
and lashed my bare legs,
frost nipped and stinging.

I can still picture my father leaning into the forceful
gales
holding the crown of his brown fedora with one hand,
the other tucked deep inside his pocket,
his old brown dress coat flapping against his wiry frame
like a wounded bird
struggling to fly.

The Cup

I think of you as I write this
with stick pens and ballpoints
that lean against the walls
of their mesh cage,
until the next flourish
of words hit the page,
until all the pages
are filled with doodles
and random thoughts
I managed to snag
as they flew by.

A dozen dog-eared bookmarks
from the last bookstore standing
in the city village
look like students
waving *pick me* with their arms
remind me
to buy a book now and then,
next year's calendar,
a magazine or two and
greeting cards for every occasion
for friends to discover in their post box

that they might tear open with an index finger
or slice along the crease with a steak knife,

like the metal hair pin engraved with a cherub holding a
flower
I found among my grandmother's things –
neatly wrapped in a fifty-year-old secret
on the page of a small-town newspaper
where drawings of leather luggage, hats, and fine
clothing
dangle under the banner of a haberdashery
bearing her name.

Playing With Fire

For his grand entrance each summer
Uncle Fred's green Chevy Coupe
blared Chuck Berry and Little Richard
from roof-mounted loudspeakers
rousing a riot of kids
slamming screen doors
high on the prospect of a street dance.

Ice cold watermelon
and Carmen Miranda pineapple
by the half-moon,
with water from hairy coconuts
cascaded down our chins.

After dinner, in our milk mustaches
and spaghetti-stained t-shirts,
we bellied up to the ticket booth
for the side yard carnival
clutching our entry fee,
a scrap of litter or bottle cap
to join the mob of kangaroos on pogo sticks,
the herd of menacing giants on wooden stilts,
or two of a dozen legs dangling between the spokes of
a wooden wagon wheel merry-go-round.

Hypnotized by quarters disappearing under a table
or behind an ear,
scarves growing out of a top hat,
The Amazing Snowball
chases a Milk-Bone biscuit
in and out of a red hula hoop
ablaze with cardboard flames.

Worn out, we dropped,
one by one, then a dozen,
but not forever, like Peggy, who watched
through the window screen
in leg braces from her wheelchair.

Magic Bullets

Doped up on placebos
and magic cure-alls,
I carry on with bravado

dreaming backwards
of sepia photographs
in gilded picture frames

to a time when hunger
was the diet plan.
Waking to relentless losses,
I wander, stymied for a solution,
telling myself stories

that once you live
inside your heartbreak,
you might settle into it
and it into you
like warm slippers and a cozy bathrobe
on frosty mornings.

But while you stand there
wrapped in a towel,
dripping with grief,
looking through the darkness
for hope and redemption
life moves on without your permission.

Just Yesterday

I woke to the reveille of your voice,
memories aroused by the call of church bells
snow glowing under lamplights,
the sweet scent of pine resin
from the fresh cut tree standing in the corner.

I sip coffee,
listen to the distant train whistle
and watch the sun rise
between the houses
beyond the weeping cherry tree

and wonder what voices Aunt Gen heard
as she set the table in the small dining room,
when at midnight she would escape
to a semi-cloistered convent.

They vanished,
bubbles poked with a pin.
All I have left
is the last handwritten letter
you wrote, still folded inside its yellowing envelope,
the foot you replaced on my music box,
and photos of everyone smiling for the camera.

They were here just yesterday,
for dinner, on some holiday
when perfumes of cinnamon and sage
diffused in the sunset-glow of the kitchen, my father's
brown dress pants were all we could see of him behind
the newspaper under the halo of the reading lamp.

Hope in a Suitcase

After shivering in the car
under the moon and starlit
Mojave Desert,
The Weight playing on the radio,
I pulled up to a California ghost town's diner
for scrambled eggs and rye toast,

joining the locals lined up
on cracked red vinyl stools
along the counter
where memories swirled
in the breeze of café ceiling fans
along with cigarette smoke and the latest gossip.

I stepped into the shade
of the abandoned movie house marquee
that read *Town Without Pity,*
a brief escape from the heat of the sun
that parched my skin
through blue jeans
and a black turtleneck.

I carry the image of my father
that morning I said goodbye—
yesterday, last week, or years ago—

when I watched from the doorway
as he sat in the kitchen
in a house not his own
calloused hands, workman's arms
forged by long labor in the open hearth.

Smoothing his thin white hair
with nicotine fingers
as if to calm the sorrow
pulling down his sunken cheeks,
his round blue eyes
speak their familiar language,
staring off
at the ticking red clock on the wall.

Girlhood

Heading out alone into the crackling night air
to sell Christmas Seals for school,
before long, snow creeps into the holes
of my rubber overshoes.
My toes ache with frostnip.

I walk along a balance beam
of ice and crusty snow
to the four-unit apartment buildings
that loom over the drab street.
I climb stairs, ring doorbells
and with one more to go

I spy the boy in the white jacket
rounding the corner
flanked by his gang
like wings on a raptor.

Ducking into an apartment building,
I climb the stairs in the dimly lit hallway.
Sensing my distress, a neighbor calls my home.

No one will come.

I return to sit in the stairway
where I study the rhythmic pace
of the boys' shadows eclipsing
the streetlamp's light on the wall,
and then

I bolt.
Into the darkness.
Through the shortcut
over the A&P parking lot
onto the busy highway
darting between cars,
hopping over snowbanks
dodging between project houses
the last 40 yards my feet barely
touching the ground.
Home free
to a family in the lamp lit living room
listening to *The Lion Sleeps Tonight*
playing on the radio
while reading the newspaper.

Only the dishes I washed hours before,
no longer dripping in their rack,
await my return.

Lungs on fire,
I sit on the basement stairs
gasping for breath.

I glance over at the window.

The boy in the white jacket stares back at me.

A Perfect Day for Wondering

First day of school for my four siblings
the only sounds were mother's footsteps,
the only movement over her swollen belly
the swing of the mop
sloshing over the linoleum floor.

In the distance, a fog horn
reverberated, guiding ore freighters
into the canal.

I make scrambled eggs in an iron skillet
before taking my place
in the smooth wooden rocking chair
Uncle Fred made in his basement workshop
for my brother, the first born,
ten years before.

By the time it got to be mine
only a few traces of paint
clung to the wood grain
and the stencil of a grinning teddy bear
in yellow overalls with orange buttons.

The seat, an obtuse angle to lean back on,
the sides, oblong, with an oval thumbhole
to grip, as some children might
the ones who care about balance and gravity.

A marvel in simplicity,
no one ever tipped backwards
though we dumped forward often enough,
squirming with laughter.

Holding teddy in my arms,
three sisters old by then,
he winked at me with one button eye,
nose missing, cotton stuffing
bursting at the seams
we rocked, taking it all in.

Notes in Isolation

When you mentioned again how we have to get
creative,
I took you up on it.
If not for the stubborn kinks in the garden hose
I could have spent the entire day
washing my bad habits down the driveway.

I take a walk with the full moon
on streets drifting off to sleep,
their flotsam and jetsam
settling in for the night,
snuggling against curbs,
napping under hedgerows,
curling up in the corners of
darkened shop doorways.

Images float and bob
like pieces of broken furniture
in knee deep waters
where I slog around,
nowhere to sit.

Even with the house under quarantine,
Mother's children
leave their rooms
to light a fire while the animals,
like our imaginations,
run wild.

Legacy

John Fox, 1857 - 1913

When my mother whispered
that her grandfather
hanged himself in the closet,
she gave me that look that said,
but we don't talk about it,
which left me wondering
if a truer story
smoldered in the dying flames
of family secrets.

After searching for his name
in the rural village records
written in flowing script,
I found, on yellowed, crisp pages,
under cause of death:
razor cut to the throat.

The lies people tell
leave gaping wounds
where shame grieves
then courses
cold
through the bloodlines
until they burst,
and splatter.

Corridors

After we picked all the meat
from the bones of our marriage,
I left the desert to its denizens
and took refuge in the house of kin
in my rusty hometown
along the shores of Lake Erie.

One summer night, too lost to go home,
those environs so distant and strange,
I stopped into a bar, for me
just another absurdity in the crucible
of going home again.

As I sipped a glass of red wine,
a man walked in with friends.
They lit up the place
with the warm glow of a swarm of fireflies.
As if we had known each other all along,
my next life began.

Four decades passed through that portal
before I went back to that bar.

A reel of vignettes flashed by:

a day at the lake
with my sister and her boyfriend—
my mother shaving cabbage on a shredder—
those summer mornings in her Victorian house
filled with the whooshing sound of the lake breeze
through the window screens.

All reclaimed by time
nothing sweet to remember.
Even the house collapsed,
its dead walls and barren rooms languish
under the rubble of apathy.

Broken In

When I went to buy a new pair of shoes
and when I could not find a good fit
the salesman said, *you have to break them in.*

Life is like that. B*reaks us in.*
We get used to things,
like my dream to go to summer camp,
not just to escape the chaos in our cramped apartment,
but to hear the quiet beauty of piney woods,
feel the solitude of lying in a sunny canoe
in the middle of a lake
with only birds and fish for company.
No money for that on my father's steelworker pay.

I joined the Girl Scouts
After I heard that kids
could earn their way to summer camp,
and sure enough, the prize that year
went to the one who sold the most cookies.

I walked miles house-to-house
in the sleet and snow to make the sales,
then back again to deliver each one
by sled or wagon
just to win my treasured prize.

The scout leader
who kept track of my tally
drove her daughter house-to-house
in their brand-new station wagon
until she sold and delivered
enough boxes of cookies
to win
by one.

April

That year, when April showed up
before the sun,
I found myself rummaging
through the drawers of time
under layers of metaphors
searching for answers
to the questions I collected
long before I was born.

The coffeepot
playing its morning tune,
the dogwalkers out
in great numbers, despite the rain,
under hoods, hats, and striped umbrellas
their charges, swaddled and dry.

While scents and aromas may evoke memories for
others,
for me, as the light falls on this cool evening
with its marching shadows,
I recall when the friend of a friend,
under the guise of a dinner date,
became the would-be rapist
I fought, and fled.

Each time I pass Elmwood and Bidwell,
I see my young self in that shop doorway
tucked into the darkest corner
with the debris,
huddled, shivering, miles away from
the house with no soul,
not far enough away from police
idling at the traffic light
dangling a nightstick out the window.

When the sun rose orange,
igniting the grass and glinting the dew,
I climbed the steps
of the dull red and silver cross-town bus
and felt eyes boring into
the dark purple bruise
on my cheek.

I warm my hands on the coffee cup
and drink to another mercurial April day,
leaving me to hope for another year
when curtains of clouds
part ways for the full Pink Moon,
and the rising Venus and Mercury
as we drift again through the comet's dusty wake
from the radiant where Lyra strums her harp
and brilliant lights hasten by.

Acoustic Shadows

I traveled the long gravel driveway
lined with ancient maples
to wait in the room
with its box of white noise
that protected the privacy of the patient inside.

Heartsore and spirit bruised
yet glad to be there
with the French healer
who helped me through the unraveling.

I watched the mango moon
rise regal on the indigo sea of starlight.
A man and woman stepped out,
we smiled, nodded,
and lingered awhile at this stoplight
on the arc of our lives.

My turn.
I found her cuing up *Claire de Lune*,
a little water music to fill the air pockets,
she said, to help me shed my disguises
and believe in happiness
while forest demons
lurked inside acoustic shadows
seen but not heard
singing off-key in misty notes
that melted into mossy carpets.

After the Reading

We gather on Winfield's
welcome mat
in the pub of good cheer
after shedding our sentiments
on the poetry floor.

I could not help seeing your fedora
dangle on the hat rack
in your after-work life,
which bar stool you chose
to shoot the breeze with workmates
over glasses of Iroquois beer,
smoking Chesterfield cigarettes
lit with the monogrammed Zippo lighter
we gave you one Christmas.

The weight of anticipation—
how fed-up Mom would be
how narrow your mood,
how icy the gale of stale words,
how my pillow muffled the sound
as the tension
pierced the marrow of my bones.

Would you recognize me,
older now than you ever grew to be?

Suspense

Furniture travels
room to room
for the men
who ply ten leaky windows
from their frames.

Dust settles on floors and tabletops
sweeps up in swirls
and now the sun lights up our days
lake breezes cool the nights
the moon watches
our reflections
where we appear
in our variegated lives
without a hint of the uncertainty

about the next doctor,
the next bit of news.

Tell us it looks good,
give us a new reason to rebel
while we make plans

to throw ourselves
a surprise party.

Hearthstone

At the open window
next to my writing table,
the earth holds my feet to the floor.
We look up where Luna waves from her chariot
rolling by the gauzy moon.

The towel you use to wipe your brow
dangles from the table,
the scent of honeysuckle
in the night air

mingles with familiar voices
from stoops and porches, floats inside,
settling on the bare wooden floors.

In your wake,
the cat hightails it
from room to room
prancing in gray and white
from one century into the next
without a single resolution,
snubbing his nose at the ancient tradition
to appease the gods of Babylon.

Through the fog of shadows,
a dog walker appears
in the spray of the streetlamp
then disappears
like Jimmy Durante
bidding goodnight to Mrs. Calabash
before walking away through circles of spotlights
on the darkened stage.

We savor the seasonal sojourn
where waters wash up along
our northeastern shore.
Too swiftly the summer
that solstice ushered in
hands over the keys
to autumn, and its equinox.

Starting Over, Again

After your call caught me
in a tangle of tricks and guile,

I wrapped my skin
in a blanket of stars

around a ball of moon
and found a moment of peace.

Then, when morning appeared
in her yellow dress

to walk with me into the past
over miles of slippery rocks,

I hoped I might find you there,
at the baptismal font of truth and forgiveness.

The Cat's Apprentice

The runt born in a horse barn
without papers or pedigree
pushed from the nest too soon
mewled louder
until it melted just one heart

for a lifetime of laser beams,
sparkly balls, squeaky mice,
and fishing poles of feathers and carrots
to spar with.

He demands a dripping faucet
by yowling from the bathroom,
raised windows for bird watching through screens,
and seven pounds of roadblock
in the kitchen doorway
to stare into a bowlful of soft food
for an order of more gravy.

Why have a laptop
just sitting
on a lap if not to climb over
and back again,
then again,
and back, and again,

if not to settle
into the narrow space
between armrest and thigh?

Two black circles peer out
from a snowy mug of fur
beckoning me to drop everything
for a few head scratches,
one slow stroke from head to tail,
and a neck massage
until he nods off
and all the tensions of my day
flit and flicker like sparks
from a smoldering campfire
that vanish into the free wind.

Captured

Kidnapped? I'm not sure
what word would describe
what happens to me,
but I can tell you,
it happens all the time.

They don't kick the doors in
and roll me up in a carpet and carry me out
and then whisper ransom demands
over the telephone at midnight.

Maybe *hijacked* is the better word,
although I'm not sure
about that, either,
since hijacks usually involve
airplanes, and I don't fly.

Abducted? How else to describe
an ordeal that occurs while sitting in a chair
in a sunlit room, or under a lamp
reading a book

that grabs me by the scruff of the shirt,
pulls me into a saga
without luggage or passport
into a foreign land
to mingle with lives lived long ago
where nothing
is lost
in the translation.

Centennial

At the first glint of sun on the horizon
when the lilt of birds rise in the trees,
I imagine walking down to the creek
that once flowed through my backyard

until a hundred years ago
when men came along
with their shovels and brawn
and buried the crystal waters

that captured the colors of the sky
dawn to dusk,
offered its fish,
watered the roots and berries,
twinkled in moonglow
of the endless turn of the seasons
as it smoothed river rock
that still charms the landscape.

News

What news do the birds relay
from treetops in their coos and chatter,
or so captivates a dog
to stake a claim with his nose
a patch of grass or a sidewalk crack
or a weed growing out of a boulder?

I snapped the rubber band
from the rolled-up newspaper
to unfurl and unfold on the table
to bring the outside world in from the cold
and hold in the palms of my hands.

Then you came along with your news
to simply say *benign,*
from its
ordered place among beautiful words
in the Oxford English Dictionary.
I crawled up to the top of the word mountain
and placed it on a golden pedestal,

then slid down the side of the rock,
leaned against it
and smiled
while the clouds rolled by
and I drank in the bright air
with my morning coffee.

The Wind

When I open the windows
to clear the air of words
we exchanged
in the heat of the moment

the wind whips through
from room to room
into shadows and corners
pushing paintings off easels
tipping floor lamps off stands
scattering papers from stacks.
Curtains snap like towels
in a locker room
knocking candles and books
off the coffee table.

The wind shoos me along
on my way to the kitchen
parts my hair down the middle
the air moist and cool
presses my dress against my back
wraps my legs in silky fabric.

The trees bend to its will.
The cat jumps to the windowsill
for a fluff of the coat
a tickle of the whiskers
and news of the roaming clowder of cats.

This Morning

The pomegranate sun dropped in from the galaxy
just in time to turn pinecones into pumpkin ornaments
dangling from the Candlewood Torch
where a Northern Cardinal
sings a hymn about the seven deadly sins and seven
heavenly virtues.

In your rainy streetscape paintings,
headlamps drip, and taillights drizzle.
From the arbor, the silver squirrel steals side glances at
me
while stuffing himself with rose hips

the cat hightails it through the house
glistening with holiday glitter
after rubbing his cologne
on the tiny European Cypress
minding its own business in a ruby red pail.

Santas, snowmen, reindeer, and nutcrackers
sleep it off on neighborhood lawns
like hungover layabouts
until electric air pumps
in charge of inflating egos
return them to their upright positions.

When a shard of refracted light bounces off the mirror,
the whole room blushes crimson
like the sweater you gave me on Valentine's Day
embroidered with stories you like to tell.

On a mesh cup where I stash my daydreams
I keep a metal pin clipped to its side
with the word *Kind* written in yellow script
on a red heart trimmed with gold.

Perhaps a thousand years from now,
the pin will rise from its earthen home,
when script will be an ancient hieroglyph,
the finder will pick it up, rub the dirt from its raised lettering,
and pin it to a mesh cup filled with daydreams.

To the Storyteller

On early Sunday morning walks
in Forest Lawn, now ablaze with colors,
we imagine the lives of the people
introducing themselves by their headstones.

We stop on the stone bridge.
White geese glide on Mirror Lake
under the watchful gaze of The Three Graces,
Aglaia, Thalia, and Euphrosyne
bathing in the fountain spray.

Under these pallid skies
where mounds of charcoal snow
refuse to leave the premises,

our words dangle like icicles
on leaky rock walls.

Leaning into the icy wind, we walk on,
warmed by the sight of the yellowing willows.

As you wonder aloud if you are ready to
let go of another member
of your flock of hand puppets—
those wild personalities you reined in,
and fastened to your repertoire until curtain call.

I picture you at your desk on a snowy evening
in the halo of the writing lamp, pen in hand
cooking up funny, vivid tales
about songbirds and birthdays
mesmerizing children big and small.

In summer we savor paths with the shadiest canopies
the cool air fragrant with pine,
dewy grass, a hint of clover,
ideal conditions for
following each other's example,
and watching
squadrons of honking geese take flight.

To Those Who Came Before

On my first trip to an antique shop
I accept an invitation
from a settee
born in the era of serious people and furniture--
to rest on her light of heart, shameless dress
in colors of whimsy and sunshine
while she ignores the disapproving eye
of wood trim
in the shape of a handlebar mustache
and the hoo-ha of Suffragettes
lingering in her cushions.

All my senses captured by these designs
crafted long before
I left the small homely rooms,
the stormy place with angry walls

where we bobbed and floated,
unmoored by love, and the dimensions of history.

Now I live in a house where two sisters
listened to the same
creaking floorboards underfoot,
woke to the same hissing radiators
warming the darkness
on shivery winter mornings,

read by lamplight
next to the same bookcases,
breathed sweet bouquets of fruit pies
cooling on the same windowsill,
and rested in the ambiance
of the same neon sunrays
and chalky moonbeams
bursting through
the same wavy window glass.

Ode to the Newspaper

In the early hours
when the sun was barely
up to her eyebrows in horizon,
newspapers hit the front door with a thud
bringing wakefulness to households,
neighbors in robes and pajamas
popping out like figurines in a cuckoo clock
to read the blaring headlines on the doorstep
thrown there by the paperboy
pulling his green wooden delivery wagon.

An ordinary ritual by ordinary people
that spoke a common language
they drank in, deeply,
with their morning coffee—
news with facts and context,
poetry that took us down dark or candlelit passageways,
sports, the clever game by inches
and opinions, clearly marked, on their own page.

How I loved lying on the floor
leaning on my elbows,
fascinated, horrified, delighted,
and in a grand semicircular sweep,
turning the page
with fingers blackened with ink,
whole columns tattooed on my arms.

It went on like that for years
until I washed my hands of it all
in the bathtub, after the words turned cold and flat
unable to resist the tug of rapids
pulling civility
down the drain with the bathwater.

Connection

On a Sunday afternoon
downtown,
under the baking sun
where desperation
loiters on deserted streets,
my car idles at the stoplight
across from the City Mission.

A war veteran,
draped in fatigue,
waits on the corner
in the sliver of shadow
cast by the stem of a streetlamp.

We glance at each other
through my open car window.
His eyes hold me in a soft gaze
over the canyon of our worlds
as he teeters on the rim
between here and hell.

Time

Microwaves nuke the seconds
ovens bake the minutes
church bells toll the hours
atoms clock the days
calendars march along
month by month
ball drops ring in the years
songs reminisce the decades

we count ourselves
by the number of birthdays
in a lifetime
as time crawls up our bodies
and steals

what made us
what got us through.

Pilgrimage

Life is a long lesson in humility. –Sir James M. Barrie

If your life begins where birds land in the lilac tree
and sing for you outside the sunny window,

eventually you may tumble down the stairway of life
leaving scraps of birthright in the corners,
your entitlements wedged in scruffy grooves,
the safety of banisters and newel posts
broken out and used for firewood,
and the floor of security warped,
on the verge of collapse.

As Proverbs says, …*with humility comes wisdom.*
Though you may have a new pair of eyes
to see the world,

if your stairway
begins on concrete and asphalt
and home is a third-floor walk-up
with gang tags and graffiti climbing the walls
to a musty flat, days filled with hunger and want,
dog-eared furniture fading under the glare of a bare
lightbulb—

what long lesson awaits you?

Culture Wars

I often wake up to words banging on dictionary gates,
running through tunnels looking for an escape hatch
where they emerge
out of my retractable ballpoint pen gliding along
the postcard from Niagara Falls,
or seeping through my fingertips
onto the keyboard,
to mix and mingle on the screen,
to convene on a cloud
then settle in
to serve out their sentence.

On dark winter mornings,
I hear the growing pile of books
chatter as they teeter on the corners of my desk
groans from the ones crammed into bookshelves
who arrived clean-shaven, trimmed and crew-cut
now dog-eared, weak-spined,
fluttering with bookmarks.

Then, the irony of the orphans
scattered on the floor,
the guides that help me
find my way home in the dark,
seem to grow in quantities
without a permanent place to be.
I tiptoe out of the room,
careful not to step on their feelings.

Meanwhile, well into the afternoons,
lyrical notes sleep it off
oblivious to the din of paints squeezing
out of tubes for the artist
who translates a surly winter landscape
into the silent language of pigments and polychromes
then tones things down for the road trip
where I lose all perspective
and disappear into the vanishing point.

Stormy Monday

This morning I wrote two thank you notes
on wisps of white paper,
one in a poem, the other in the first person
as if I were the amber glass pen
in the shape of a tendril
pirouetting across the page.
While waterlogged clouds
couldn't make up their minds
to flurry, sleet, or downpour,
and the wind banged on the windows,

I left the house to join the dog walkers
blowing down the street
with dogs that tug and tarry
for just one more sniff
before trotting off to the next inquisition
on slushy foot paths
lined with tufts of snow.
My icy toes protest in leaky boots.

I chat with the neighbor
who lives in the yellow house across the street
walking his tiny white poodle
in red woolen wrapping.
We gaze at dead stalks in the drifts
over the garden beds,
the heralds of spring.

We agree to start counting the days.

Inside the warm house through the side door,
my soggy boots collapse on themselves,
and my coat, drenched and heavy on its hanger,
drips and puddles on the basement floor.

I run upstairs toward the sound of sirens
see lights flashing outside the front windows
where medics carrying heavy bags park their gurney
at the landing, rush up the steps of the blue house two
doors down.
My neighbor, the Army veteran with the kind eyes,
has fallen asleep forever.
What are cold toes to me now?

Still

In these parts, the mills that fell to ruins
have been reborn
as domiciles
as hallowed ground
sanctuary for dreamers
bird land
wind farm
canvas for the graffiti artist
solitude for aesthetes
through colonnades of doorways
on carpets of sun and shadow
over rubbled concrete
where the orphans of industry
speak in still life
under the artist's gaze.

Impact

As sullen clouds melt into wisps of white apron strings,
I walk through spindles of shade on the sidewalk
amid people leaving their homes on foot,
on bicycles, with dogs on the leash.

I hear the loud thud of a truck that stops dead,
smashes into a man on his bike
the bike smashes into the curb,
the man skids across the lane like a base runner
diving into home plate.
His eyes meet mine, he says, *I'm okay.*
Lying in the street,
he slips into his work phone,
calls the boss at the big box store,
says, *I'm sorry.*

Even as sirens blare
from fire trucks and police cars,
after the ambulance arrives with its rescue team
he still inhabits his phone
scared, desperate,
reassuring his boss
acting as if nothing had happened,
as if he will show up later
after this brief interruption.

People spill out of stores to take a look,
like a flock of hovering hummingbirds
wondering in whispers
about the man with the phone
whose voice trails off
as the lock clicks
on the ambulance doors.

The bike's inner tube escapes from its tire
like a ringneck snake
slithering from under a rock
bulging with prey
bang!
explodes.

Heartland

I wish you could have seen
the plowers and sowers in straw hats
and frayed overalls flock to local diners
for crackly sermons from a.m. radios

preaching farm reports as the sun tipped its hat
on the morning side of the round earth.

After rye toast and eggs,
I surfed the waves of country roads,
a gang of birds tagging along as if I were
the purveyor of worms and seeds

and not the idle tourist
taking in the sweet powdery scent
of canola in bloom on rolling
patchwork quilts

where conventions of dairy cows
in black and white
fan themselves under shade trees
and lift their heads if only
to wrap me in their soulful gaze.

I wish I had a traveling companion
like Steinbeck had Charley,
not just for his agreeable face with cheerful eyes
or the rhythm of his ears flapping in the wind

but to share the poetry in those whistle-stops
where the song of ants and worms
plowed the belly of the brown earth
and the hum of load-bearing bees
were lyrical prayers of our daily bread
from the church of the abundant harvest.

The Beauty of Night

Almost home—
where the glow from my desk lamp
beckons me to climb the steps,
wrestle with the old loose doorknob,
fall into the arms of a warm quiet,
free from bombs, guns,
nature's tantrums—

I mourn lives lost,
strewn in the ashes and rubble,

and my departed friends
as our generation
marches ever closer to the edge.

Home in time to watch night fall
on the urban street
from the safety of my aqua room
with its *Ocean Boulevard* wall paint
I reminisce
about my existence narrowed down
to the hours in a workday

when I closed off the sun
peering in through the office window

and drew the blinds to the poetry of night
as if to ward off the hunters
who keep us walled in
and separate even from ourselves

the music in the trees,
the stillness of the moon
among swarms of stars bursting in and out,
buzzing by,
the fragrance in November's air
wafting up from leaves disturbed by footfalls
on sidewalks
buried
under the crisp debris of autumn.

Life Without Parole

No shame for the men
who drank
scotch in the office,
or knackered by noon
after a three-martini lunch
at the country club,
or guzzled boilermakers at the bar
after a shift
at the factory.

But if you were locked in the prison
of domesticity,
ordered beer by the case,
drunk by afternoon,
and on balmy summer days
sat on the stoop
in your bra and panties,
delicate, beautiful
and felt the scorn of the other prisoners
who peeked through café window curtains
watching you drown.

As the haze dimmed,
you entered the house,
climbed to the top of the stairway
where, behind closed doors,
your daughter found comfort in books,
your son took refuge from the bullies.

Through the shaded windows,
your cries from solitary
detonated the peace
of the silent afternoon.

The Visitors

On the day the earth stood still
I was in the kitchen
baking a lemon tart with a buttery crust
when the aroma from the oven
sent me adrift to the long-forgotten.

Wandering from room to room
I daydreamed of places I can no longer go
where willows dip their toes in the river
next to the No Wading sign.

Since I won't be seeing your
bouquet of faces under the porch light
anytime soon, chattering behind the window glass,
no mob of boots tussling on the welcome mat,
no scarves dangling from their wire trapeze,
no garlands of melted snowflakes
glistening on woolen coats, instead, I will wait beneath
the ticking clock
while the house whispers and hums
while the patter of paws descends the wooden staircase
until the phone pings—
and there you will be
materializing in liquid crystals
shrink-wrapped from the pixel store
warbling through electroluminescent wires.

Longevity

Ornithologist Chandler Robbins
strapped a band around
a Laysan Albatross in 1956
and named her *Wisdom.*

That was 3 million miles ago,
and she was married by then—
raising a chick on the backbone of heaven
amid the din of birds.

The two gliders set off on a whirlwind tour
swooping down on lissome wings
to catch a meal, then catch a breeze
dreaming bird dreams on nonstop flights.

I wonder where Wisdom was
when Chandler Robbins' heart stopped at age 98,
if she grieved, if she wonders where she will be
when her heart stops, who will carry on,
and who will grieve?

Going Solo

When you brought the news
that the floor fell out of your world

I was sitting on the porch in the summer heat
with a picture in my head of your biggest life as a
couplet,
and now it is not.

The tone of our conversation
felt like a funeral parlor
in a fog of pastels and sorrow

where the soul of your life
floats by, refusing to disappear.

Birthday

The apparition of your red scarf
waves in the wintry bluster
as you enter our small doorway
bathing in the entryway light,
melting snow dripping
from the hem of your coat,
pooling on the old tile floor.

We don't have a life like yours—
all the pots bubbling over,
your children, your office, your unsettled divorce.

After all these months,
laid siege by two bullies,
COVID and winter—
pushing us inside, slamming the door

we feast with joy
on your smiling eyes.

You walk into the room with a cloth bag
heavy with potted yellow tulips and purple crocuses
poking through loamy soil,
and a snowy Phalaenopsis orchid,
a flutter of angels on the wing
cinctured in their tall cellophane house
tied with chromatic ribbons,

a birthday card tucked inside its red envelope,
a bottle of wine to share, and an apology,
as if love were a train that you missed
under the ticking clocks on the wall.

Early Corn

Despite our selective breeding
we still look very off-season
our tufts of silky yellow strands
sticking out of husky green coats
toes freezing in a box of ice
as the caravan of cart pushers
so blithely pass us by
rejecting the notion
that too soon summer
will fall into the arms of autumn.

Under Heaven

In the church of Baruch de Spinoza,
the sacred lives in leaves and water,
the sweet breath of lilacs,
in the gospel according to lime green trees waving
through fences in small city yards,
beaches hugging the lake's tidy shores
to the hymn of lapping waves.

Here, birdsong is scripture.
Sermons come in happy yips from the puppy next door
who evangelizes in exclamation points
calling me to open the lattice gate
where he anoints me with kisses.

You will find the God of Spinoza
in the comfort and joy of a friend's embrace,
on a walk in the open air,

not hiding in motel room nightstands,
or sleeping on wooden pews
in brick and mortars where men
preach from lecterns and pulpits
sometimes under the gaze of granite angels and marble
saints
where the blood of martyrs stains glass windows.

Dancing With the Cardinal

You charm me awake
on golden summer mornings
with your aria
from the limb of the rescued ash tree
so your bright orange beak
will go on glowing
in the spotlight of a sunbeam
among thickets of green
as you call out to your handsome beau
with the blazing red plumage.

You wait for me to freshen the gurgling fountain
so you can land on the brim to drink
and bathe your tawny feathers
and this we will do until the season ends
when you become the bright amber star
over the realm of winter's gray and gloom.

February

When the landscape
outside my window changes
from a barroom brawling blizzard before
settling into silent satiny drifts,
and the ash tree
extends an olive branch
to a dispassionate sky

I revisit the pages of *War and Peace*
where Russian aristocrats of Tolstoy's imagination
lived under the same icy cloak

as red lights atop cell towers
glimmer like rubies in a celestial tiara
of the Empress consort,
the moon an elegant pendant
nestled in the hollow of the horizon.

Finishing Off

In the room where the windows
are rippled with age,
geranium stalks
grasp at the stoic sky.
Rain sends word
of an impending blizzard.
The wind will not long
be silent in the trees
whose dead foliage
shelters the soft earth
and its seedy underworld.

As the protagonist
in my flowing velvet cape
of Black Forest green,
I wait for words
to invite themselves in
to help me finish this poem
where the sweet
and palatable moral
will be revealed
only after I am declared victor
over some raffish cad.

Always hopeful,
I look up and down the lonely street
of shuttered windows and empty sidewalks
I feel the winds that picked up a chill
over the frozen lake,
watch them sweep away autumn's leavings,
and toss and whirl snowflakes
like dust on a breeze in a sunbeam.

Your Language in Colors

In the warmth of a sunbeam,
my amber glass pen dipped in the inkwell,
I thought of how
your devotion cannot be weighed
as wife, mother, sister, friend,
nor dutiful daughter
who saw your mother and father
off on their voyage to the everlasting
how the soul pours out of your portraits—
music in a child's eyes,
caretaker in denim overalls surveying his past,
seasoned sailor finessing the wind on the waters.

Does your eye fall upon the canvas
composing dimensions in profile and perspective
as the swirl and sweep of your hand
enunciates the complexity of character
in a visage
a gesture
the weave of cloth
before preserving its original meaning?

Here, with family and friends,
festooned in a festival of colors
of the place that, at the beginning of your journey,
opened the door
and embraced your gifts
where you taught
the language of the heart,
in stewardship of the wordless tome
a promise you kept alive—
a treasure of creativity
of imagination
and wonder,
you, the lighthouse beacon
illuminating
all those small beings
who arrived by the shipload.

Bread and Bisous

If you find yourself in Paris
in a room flooded in February sun
with doors that open onto a small balcony,
you might view a vignette
in front of a boulangerie across the street
of two men greeting each other—
you know, like those scenes in movies:
hugging and cheek kissing
to the music of happy words.

If one is holding a sack too short for a tall baguette,
he tears off a piece
and hands it to his friend,
then tears off a piece for himself
to nibble as they talk,
hands flying like maestros,
heads thrown back in laughter
as the loaf meets its crusted end.
And that, too, they share equally,
keeping the tradition of affectionate partings.

After the man with the sack
empties the crumbs onto the sidewalk
for the pigeons to peck around,
he returns to the bakery,
emerges with a warm baguette,
and stands on the sidewalk,
whistling,
waiting.

Snow Dreams

The cat curls into a nautilus
to dream near the hissing radiator.
The sunlight catches and dazzles
on whirling snowflakes
while Warren Haynes sings soulshine:
a banjo moon in a tie-dyed sky
wrapping me in a deep blue shawl.

Flighty winds
play double Dutch
with the power lines.
Gusts sculpt
drifts into cresting waves
and rattle the old wooden windows
shaking loose
their century of memories.

When my gloves stop dripping on the floor
and my toes warm in their slippers
I will dream of walking again with my beagle
still a puppy eyeing me for treats
not the scattered cloud of diamond dust
that disappeared over the horizon
into the airlight.

St. Louis Blues

I often stood alone in the shadow of Eads Bridge
watching the Mississippi
shimmer in tangerine lights
winking at me with onyx eyes

carrying the weight of its sordid past
of heartbreaks and delusions
before drifting off,
an outcast, to the open sea.

After sunset
after the heavy heat
settled like a blanket
on the bed of sleepy streets,
I walked along Laclede's Landing

where crumbling cafes served paltry promises
on balmy nights when
Billie Holiday rose from the mist
wrapped in the white gardenia air
singing *St. Louis Blues*
to the sounds of cartwheels
and the lyrical canter of horse's hooves
on the cobblestone carriageway.

Talking Walls

Instead of O'Keefe's *Blue Morning Glories*,
Cassatt's *Lilacs in a Window*,
or Kahlo's *Watermelons*

when you enter my rooms
the art on the walls will speak

through rain-soaked windshields on summer afternoons,

down a path to an abandoned farmhouse
by the light of the Milky Way,

from the lungs of the steel plant
exhaling metallic dust into copper air,

in snow drifts on oak-lined promenades
from the horse and carriage days,

among the rusty ghosts
where a squadron of gulls
reclaim industrial ruins,

through a glass door
where a pointy-eared tiger cat
dreams under a blanket of moon.

In a portrait drenched in marigold sunrise,
I lounge in a red robe
high in the heavens
dancing with the clouds,

and on a quiet night,
look down a snowy driveway
between clapboard houses,
only one spray of light
shines through a window,
and you might imagine
a figure inside, under a reading lamp
thumbing through books
on blue morning glories,
watermelons, and lilacs in a window.

The Nephew of Stars and Irises

As remnants of the Summer of Love
turned to haze in Haight-Ashbury,
on the other side of the city
I worked at a link in a hotel chain
making reservations
for wealthy world travelers
through the voices in my headset
like a zoo animal on exhibit
in a glass room that guests observed
as they ascended the escalator
to the lobby where I imagined
crystal chandeliers and white magnolias.

Hope wanes
in the dreary prison of minimum wage.
Across the continent,
my father lay dying.

Then. A man's voice wafts in over the line.
With a Dutch accent,
its timbre graying at the temples.
He asks my name, my thoughts
about the war, civil rights,
music, the social awakenings
while my pen recorded the travels he would take
with his uncle's works of art,
my memory tucked these moments away
where I keep the unforgettable.

I can still hear his words
across the decades
because you never forget
when you became visible,
when you closed the door to nowhere
and showed up for yourself.

I ask his name.
He says, *it is three words.*
He begins to spell, *V-i-n-c-e-n-t V-a-n*
I say, *the famous artist?*
He says, *oh, you know who that is?*

The Road to Hell

You could spend years living near an old couple
in the house with shiny windows
and manicured blades of grass
watch the husband
chase his lost youth in a red sports car,

his wife in a rare appearance on the back porch
shake off remnants of their lives from a small rug
and imagine the brood of children
they raised there.

After the patriarch dies,
you discover
the boat capsized long before
he abandoned ship.

Mother and her savage son
are castaways, adrift,
when an old friend moves in
drunk on a diet of whiskey
and warm smiles,
who knows if it was delirium tremens
or the unbearable anguish
wishing for death
that too soon rendered him
the shrouded figure
rolled out on a gurney

leaving mother and son
marooned again,
flailing in a rip tide.

An older son hobbled in,
long lost, dispossessed,
to lend a languid hand
but quickly bruised, banished again,
then pulled under,
found washed up,
rotting
in the wreckage
of family.

Transitions

Three decades collapse
before we meet again
at the diner with the long windows
where we gaze
into every passing face
seeking to fill our eyes
with the familiar,
with the comfort of same,
the same of being known
before we return
to each other, to lift a cup,
to swap notes,
and dust off the memory of you
in the dog-eared photograph

where it is the three of us again
where, in the milestones
we struggle to remember,
the sun catches on the band embracing
your wedding ring finger.

Wish You Were Here

Not even the restive wind
or smoldering sky
dissuades me
from this sudden lightness

when the pastels on the walls
escape from their frames
and invite me to walk
in drizzly rain
on neon streets
glowing radiant.

Reflections on glassy sidewalks
of couples, arm-in-arm
sharing secrets under an umbrella
cast in the same light
as today,
after summer
crept into the sunset
of autumn.

But that was before
I heard the news
that you drifted
into twilight
where you will always live
in the sweet scent of apples
drenching the air,
in the trill of a house wren
beholding the caramel moon.

World Cup

On this dusty globe
eight billion of us
bob in a teacup of sea
where the cosmos awaits
a reckoning
of all the kafala bones scattered
on the altar of steel boxcars
under the torch of sun.

We rock and heave
spotlit in still life
on a broken porcelain saucer
where a half-eaten crust of bread
rests in a crowd of crumbs
on silky rainbow scarves

cascading like Victoria Falls
where a glint of light
paints small windows
onto a lazy bouquet of figs

and glances off the rim
of a Champagne flute
while we float along
weighing our fate
under a worried moon.

All I Can See

In the room of windows
where the cat naps in his chair,
yellow tulips rise
on slender stems
above their lush forest,
then glow fluorescent
when the sun bursts in.

I gaze at the person I once was
in the painting by the door
where you captured the light and mood
of an ordinary moment
in an extraordinary way
curled up on the sofa
cloud watching
in my pink dress and dark brown hair
covered in tiger shadows
and sun rays.

The silver filigree suncatcher
with its star points, crescent moon,
the tiny bell dangling off the end
and small sapphire globes
dance to the song of the house sparrow.

In the middle of this plague
I find solace in the row of your medicine bottles
gathering dust now;

joy in a friend's voice, a handwritten letter in the
mailbox,
the way the lavender hyacinths endure,
their fragrance lingering,
rescued from the snow drift in the flower garden.

Cloudburst

When I stepped outside this morning
my eyes drifted up to a wispy
white cloud in the shape of a cat

not the same shape as the clouds of cat hair
that settle in the corners
and stick to the broom bristles

or clouds of dandelions gone to seed
and offered up to the wind,
or clouds of smoke from winter's chimney

but a cat god of ancient Egypt
lying on the floor of the sky like the Great Sphinx of
Giza

gazing at the angels gathered on a swing
legs dangling, robes flying, wings aflutter,
with tremendous clouds of hair, like
King Louis XIV or Marie Antoinette

a cloud that will sweep me off my feet
one with a silver lining
that I can poke my head into when I daydream

luminous puffs in lacy gowns, waltzing.

Dreams and Distractions

Time was, a map was a thing to be done with
after the trip,
a crumpled chart of memories
in food stains, coffee rings,
inked-in routes, circled landmarks, off the beaten paths,
telephone numbers, random notes, and a confusion of
creases
that served as the official record
of every failed attempt at refolding.

I look up from my map reading
to watch the cat on a reconnaissance mission
behind the gossamer curtain
eyeing the trio of blue candles
next to the window
where prisms from the blue crystal suncatcher
dance on the wall.

The car sits in the driveway,
our suitcases gather dust in the closet,
and next to the atlas,
tall spines of travel guides and
crossword puzzles
lean against the wall
in their starched uniforms
waiting for the service bell.

Early Summer Evening

Thunder clouds roll in,
wind turns the maple leaves underside out.
The bedroom darkens
but for the flickering candle
wrapping the room in a yellow shawl.

While the pot of vegetable soup simmers,
I thumb through my lifetime of photographs
and there you are, aglow,
in your couture evening dress.
Swiss Miss, we called you.
Did your Belgian prince ever send for you?
Your name has disappeared,
along with the French interpreters by your side
in their custom-made suits and chiseled faces
in that city I left so many years ago.

The sky is of two minds now,
one with clouds, the other, not.
The wind, barely a whisper.
The cardinals return to nesting,
the sun to its horizon,
and the soft rain to its watering.

Garden Church

When the wooden gate
in the backyard swings open,
though I never know what the birds have in store,
I am hardly surprised, as if by some miracle
among the thorny crowns of pink climbing roses,
the resurrection of a new branch in cardinal red.

In the garden bed, clay pots
stuffed with geraniums and vines congregate
under the priestly gaze of jack-in-the-pulpit.

Columbine bells caught in the rapture
of the lilac's bouquet
chime in an ivory vase.

Climbing hydrangeas, purple clematis
and a host of hostas
meditate in the shadowy sanctuary
of the cathedral oak tree.

A choir of wrens
sing from their nest in the cloister
over the lattice arch.
Robins bathe in the bowl of a
carved stone baptismal font.

My friend and I, delighted to be lucid and upright,
lob words across the patio table,
escape into the small of each other's lives, and
consecrate our friendship
with a communion of unleavened bread
and a chalice full of wine.

Garden Sitting

I lean back in my chair
and close my eyes
to concentrate
on the gurgle of the fountains
as if I am next to a creek
or maybe a waterfall,
in the shallows, after a drought.

Bursts of coral and blue pink impatiens
fan themselves in the shade
of the ash tree
where the shale rock path
descends from the gate
for friends and critters
to come for a visit.

The August sun shines through
the archway of bushes and trees
that keep vigil over our small city yards
until the changing of the guard
when darkness comes,
when thin ropes of lights
fool the worms with their warm glow.

Autumn arrives not when the calendar says so
but when the first seed from the ash tree
christens the yard or garden path
and the leaf of a distant tree turns gold.

The wooden man dressed in electric blue
yawns after a long day
watching the sun
arc across the sky
as it heads into the horizon
where it will spend the day
illuminating the ancient Grecian ruins,
and shedding light on a newly discovered
chamber among the Great Pyramids of Giza.

Go Somewhere

In dark times,
find a speck of light
beyond the horizon,
a galaxy away,
and steer your threadbare sanity
toward memories of peace.

Cling to the small and routine:
follow the sun beyond the river bend
listen to the music of wind blowing
through leafless trees.
Watch the sky play on its sloshy canvas,
join the waves in their resistance.

Take a journey
with a friend into terra incognita,
slip in and out of risk and uncertainty.
Stop along the way to share a dream sandwich
and dine on each other's promises.

Wander through flamboyant
landscapes on the walls,
waltz with sheer curtains,
sashay in the fan's breeze.

Relive those moments
where your stories are
marigold moonsets,
summer's first embrace
of cool water on hot skin.

Remember what came before,
when we kept the doors wide open
in case visitors wished to come through
with their radiant smiles
and the balmy scent of friendship.

Goodbye

Through the back window,
dripping with melting snowflakes,
peaks and gables
pierce the low sky like a young mountain range.

Silky scarves of smoke slip out of brick chimneys
and vanish in the silver air.

The Eastern White Pine
rises above the garage peak
like an evergreen crown—
as if the nesting cardinals
performed the ceremony.

Windows glowing amber
gaze out from spectacle-wearing dormers,
icicle earrings glint and dangle
in the light of the rising moon.

A huff of wind blows across a sloped roof
sending snow swirling like a flying skirt.

Just beyond bare brambles on the arbor,
the crest of the work shed
peeks through the lattice for a last goodbye
before closing up shop for the winter.

With curtains drawn and windows gone dark
all that's left are blinking stars, a flickering candle,
and eyelids closing as we drift off to sleep.

Here to There

The sparrow left her roost
to whistle *Ode to Joy*
on the garage roof, beckoning me with onyx eyes
to take off my slippers, blow out the candle,
and venture into the gloom and drizzle

as I once did, on slippery slopes
where foggy mists settled on the city of hills
under the dominion of clanging street cars
and pigeons on the take—

from my prison of small means
where I dreamt of blue taffeta ribbons
marking pages in leatherbound textbooks.

Now, peering from beneath
the moat sloshing in the eave of my hat

I spot children rounding the corner,
laughing and puddle-splashing,
with nothing on their minds but
winning the race against time

while a man, checking his watch,
plows into a bustling band of browsers
before disappearing through a gauntlet
of urban shop windows.

Horse Chestnut Trees

I often wonder who thought to bestow
along this urban road
émigrés from the Balkan forests
that flutter and hold sway,
and that I water occasionally, on behalf of the clouds,
just to be under their spell.

Spring drama unfolds
purple buds yawn and stretch,
tiny leaves hide behind mother's apron
the naked tree
shows up in lavish plumage

the scent of vanilla and honey
incandescence fills the air
triple scoop ice cream cones
dangling like ornaments
serving up nectar and pollen
to nature's winged agents,
before going off to dance
with every cool breeze that comes along.

Settled in for the summer,
casting shadows over villagers and voyagers,

these broad-leafed matriarchs
in their secret village
below the pavements
exchange recipes and dish the dirt,
whispering to us in hues of blue and green,
lustrating blades of grass,
and flowers in their beds.

In the Quiet

I shuffle around in my bedroom slippers
by the light of the streetlamp
in the quiet of too early darkness

the music that soaking coffee beans
make when they ping into the glass globe
sending their fragrance up the wooden staircase.

The scene beyond the window
snuggles beneath a shawl of snow

the sky settles in for last curtain call
for the traveling minstrel show
of fading starlets serenading the moon
with their song of tomorrow.

Glass snowflakes dangle in the window,
dance with light from the streetlamp
casting prisms against the wall
for the cat who waits for the seasons to revolve,
when the sunny air is warm again
when his dreams return to mice and shadows
in the small world he stands watch over,
from the wide window sill
behind the mesh screen.

In Winter

I started to write you a letter,
but mostly I stare out the window
at dull brown trees turning up their collars
against icy drizzle
thinking what more to say

about the masks we wear
and when can we leave the house again.

What difference does it make now
when I can no longer reach you
by envelope and postage stamp?

I will see you next spring, though,
in the pink roses crawling up the trellis,
in the maddening political landscape,
and when the robins return, to awaken spring at sunrise.

Lost

When your mind took up residence
on the other side of town,
I did what many of us do,
try like hell with my helmet and flashlight,
crawling through caves
and tunnels to rescue you
from a cruel destination.

No one tells us it's a fool's errand
traipsing around in a cluster of words
searching for the right one
just to keep going

even when we know
this rite of passage
is a one-way trip
through a door
dangling on its hinges.

Memorial Park

On the winding, rolling roads
draped in emerald tree shadows
a coyote stops
at the sound of a distant voice
in his ears the shape of calla lilies
before he trots off
to get what he came for.

He sneaks up on the fawn
standing alone behind an obelisk,
no fight, no struggle, no noise
just death in the cemetery.

Mallards ignore my stare
and carry on
in black and tan tweed,
grand marshaling
a dozen ducklings
flanked by a squadron of white geese
in the creek shallows
dunking for weeds and crustaceans.

A shiny black hearse
rounds the corner
crunches stones beneath its wheels
a bronze casket in silhouette
festooned with gladiolus
behind ivory curtains
as the man in the dark suit
commands a caravan
obeying the protocol
of high beams and funeral flags
on the slow roll.

A deer family
grazes on grass,
steps gently
over the garden of souls
sleeping in their beds
below granite headboards.

Take Your Pick

When you breathe in the sweet powdery scent
of canola in bloom on rolling patchwork quilt farmland
in Iowa,
does it smell like spun gold?

When you hear the song of a cardinal
do you dream of bright red feathers
among a thicket of grey leafless trees?

What do you see when you run your hands
on the smooth bark of the weeping cherry tree,
or the pale skin of water lilies?

Can you imagine that mint green 1939 Packard
with canary yellow leather seats
I saw at a car show in Mark Twain's hometown?

When you eat a midsummer peach
freshly fallen ripe off the tree,
is it blushing with autumn hues?

When you listen to the symphony of droplets
from the trees after a sun shower,
or laugh so hard the heat rises in your cheeks
and tears gather in your looking glass eyes,
can you feel them shimmering?

Morning Light

I get up early on summer mornings
to watch life unfold,

the trill of the birds
how the trees own the landscape
their leaves cooled
by the still dewy air.

The sun dapples the shady yard
flowers ask for watering
the shale path for sweeping,
and beyond the lattice gate,
the backyard neighbor rests on a chair
in her patio garden
wondering.

Morning

My bedroom slippers
shuffle along the floorboards
interrupt the stillness

then coffee pings into the glass globe
sending its fragrance up the wooden staircase.

Beyond the window
above the shawl of snow

settling in for last curtain call
for the traveling minstrel show,
fading starlets sing their song of tomorrow
to the man in the moon.

Glass snowflakes dangle in the window.
By the looks of things, redundant to passers-by
not privy to their primary function
of throwing prisms against the wall
keeping the cat occupied until
the seasons revolve, when the sunny air is warm again
when his dreams return to mice and shadows
in the small world he stands watch over,
from the wide window sill
behind the mesh screen.

On My Watch

The candy-colored prism
splays on the floor
in a different kind of silence
than the stunt Harold Lloyd pulled
dangling from the clock
over Hollywood movieland.

I can't hear the screams
over the roar of barbaric lawnmowers
of grass blades
shredded by the thousands
on shadowed lawns
all over the neighborhood.

The sliver of amber moon
sleeps in its midnight blue bedroom
framed in perfect harmony
with ash and oak trees

and power lines
whose main public utility
serves as a perch for the songbirds
and a highway for squirrel traffic.

The cat sleeps in his paper bag
under the table.
Peaches ripen in their glass bowl.
August air
waltzes through the house
as the call of mothers in treetops and doorways
beckon their children
home for the night.

Painting with Music

Colorless clouds erase every breath of blue,
ivory hydrangea blossoms overwinter
in a velvety blend of clove and cinnamon
climb over aging cedar lattice,
casting lavender shadows
on fractured asphalt.

The wind, a bored adolescent,
pelts raindrops against the windows
while you clang a metal spatula against an iron skillet.
Whatever you've got sizzling in there
teases me with aromas I can't yet name.

Dabbing the floor with his paws, the cat sings
musical poetry of Pythagoras and Euripides
ancient rhythms in a tradition
that he's been carrying around for 2,000 years
and still remembers how to play.

Drowned out by its loud, dissonant music of heartbeats,
the whole planet comes and goes
thumping with life
except the flowers dangling
over the sides of the vase,
and the fly lying on its back on the windowsill.

Picture Postcards

When you wrote about strolling
along the rues of Paris
with your head full of currencies and idioms,
did they resemble the walks we took
to the hardware store
where our conversations
flowed down the aisle like a lazy river?

Did you get home in time to catch the afternoon sun
as it barged through the open window
and set ablaze the sunflowers in their fluted vase?

Remember those glass orbs on sticks?
Well, they still light up the flower garden
with their alluring gaze
and sunny dispositions.

The only thing missing from that scene
on the balcony under a jasmine arbor
overlooking the Mediterranean
was you, in your white sun dress
sipping a glass of wine the color of garnets.

Forgive me the ink smears.
You know how enthusiastic
juicy oranges are this time of year
leaving us humbled
by their pleasing personalities,

unlike the obstinate grapefruit
I wrangled with this morning,
tearing at its flesh to get to the good stuff—
pulp thick with pucker tart juice.
P.S. I didn't even mind the squirt in the eye.

Reverie

Roaming the streets
of the artisan village
I search for a bohemian or two
with a map in their heads
willing to take me on a guided tour of roads to the past.

Imagining in the garden on early summer evenings
my grandmother tats a linen handkerchief
as we sway gently on the porch glider
surrounded by pink, red, and coral geraniums
sunning themselves on the railing.

I found among my grandmother's things
a collection of hand-carved buttons
in Currier & Ives cookie tins
remnants of a life
in velvet, crepe, and taffeta.

Buskers owned the sidewalks then.
Smoke wafting from taverns made you high,
nobody bothered to sweep doorways
or dispatch shop window displays
crammed with dusty antiques and tins full of buttons.

Sleepy Morning

I wake to the lingering scent of honeysuckle
from last night's candle, the one that rescues
my mood on moonless nights.
A fugue of raindrops glance off the eaves,
play on the frozen pond,
like ice fishermen poking holes
in its shiny surface.

I close my eyes and dream of Amsterdam.
Along the canal under lamplight,
I settle at a sidewalk café
for a slice of edam and walnut bread,
and a pint or two.
A couple asks to join me.
We exchange smiling glances
across the round glass table.
New joiners rearrange the furniture
until we are a swirl of moons
glowing like stars
on a map of constellations.

After we part,
I make a soft landing from my dreamscape,
homesick for the smell
and sound of coffee
gurgling in its pot.
I watch the cardinal,
crimson against the pewter sky,
trying again this year to test his weight
on the bare branches of the oak sapling
before flying off to sing for his mate
atop the towering maple.

Small World

A cavalry of blackbirds secures the high ground
on a 40-foot hollowed-out K-Mart sign,
the long-abandoned standard-bearer of a two-acre
parking lot
where buttercups and dandelions hibernate
under cracks in the blacktop,

and while murderous chaos explodes in the streets,

we still have the symmetry of butterfly wings,
Jupiter and Saturn aligned, once in a hundred blue
moons,
the rhythm of waves washing up on a beach
in the morning stillness.

Surrounded by Angels

Your angel might show up -
not in the Book of Ezekiel
but at the front door -
holding a paper plate
full of pastel-colored French pastries
with stories of christening her new oven,
though not, as you might imagine:
barefoot in flowing ivory robes
with a halo shining above her crown
standing over a baptismal font brimming with holy
water.

Or there may be two
who will not appear as
heralds flying across the dome of a basilica
summoning you to the everlasting,
but voices over the telephone
calling to ask how you are,
and after a friendly exchange,
send you on an errand
to find artisan bread, homemade soup, pasta sauce,
and a wedge of your favorite cheese
waiting outside the door.

Instead of feathery wings and a wistful gaze,
she will be a reincarnation
in a ponytail and complexion illuminated by
a windbreaker the color of buttercups
who brings not a mound of hosts hidden inside a
ciborium
or a chalice filled with table wine,
but a loaf of banana bread that
serves as both food and fragrance
to share with you
and maybe a few ancestors,
at the altar
of reverence and the quiet mind.

The Hawk

When I told you
what I saw
that morning
in the graveyard
among the amber groves
shedding their seeds and robes

how the red-tailed hawk flew
so close she filled my eyes
with chocolate cinnamon plumage,
brown suede wings
and black velvet fringe
I had only seen in photographs

I did not tell you that when
she plucked the squirrel from its branch

how it felt to be part of something solemn
and violent,
I could not walk away from
without honoring death

with a kaleidoscope wreath
of nature's painted debris

against the base of the tree
mourning the loss of its villager.

The Visitor

Although I don't mind
you just dropping by,
thanks for giving me time
to sew up the holes in my story,
close the book on all those half-read magazines,
and fluff up the pillows and memories
before we redecorate the room
with our frame of mind.

We fall into conversation
listening to words beyond their meaning.
Thoughts tucked inside each other
like paper airplanes fly between us
with no estimated time of arrival.

Now that all the bills are paid
the larder stocked
the roof high and dry
the wolf abandoned the door

the cat's sleeping in the window
and all there is to count
is a houseful of blessings
and pens full of ink.

Tomorrow

I called the vet to reorder
the cat's monthly dose of pills.
They will be waiting for me in the morning
in a white paper bag labeled *Rudy*.
I order ahead so I will not be among the people
waiting on the row of chairs
that line the walls
staring into space
though I will smile as I walk past
the cats peering through mesh screens
from one of those trendy pouches
that come in an array of fall colors
that, when lined up, remind you of the calendar photo
of October in the Berkshires,

and grin at the hounds and retrievers
sitting tall and still on their haunches
the way dogs do when they are spring-loaded rockets
ready for take-off,
ears rotating in half arcs
searching for a signal,
watching,
noses atwitch and sensate,
rivulets of drool dangling
from dewlaps
and pooling on the tile floor.

I will smile and thank the assistant
who slips me the bag
under the plastic Covid shield,
before I duck out quickly.

Next stop is the pet store,
avoiding the aisle of living creatures—
the rescue cats in roomy apartments,
rabbits and gerbils in glass habitats,
and aquariums and terrariums
full of fish and amphibians.

I will wind my way to the cat toy section,
to replace the laser beams
gone dark after endless hours playing dart and dash.
It is the least I can do
for an animal confined to the same rooms
all day, all week, all year, for years on end,
nineteen, to be exact,
rescued as a runt from a horse barn.

Turning

In the early evening when my boots grow weary,
I return to the warmth of my solitary room,
fragrant with white hyacinth in a glass vase,
a painting of peaches from last summer's harvest,
my woolen coat, caught in a snowstorm,
drips on the tile floor.

Without the discipline of schedules,
the walls of structure fall away,
inviting the luxury of sitting a spell,
while the past, with its liquid ghosts,
appears and disappears
along the waterways of memory.

Should a quote by a famous author happen by,
it won't be long before yardsticks
from the Ministry of Measurements show up,
in their starched shirts and bow ties,
to chastise me for all the books I failed to read.

I wonder if I will be more or less
after interrogating myself
under a bare lightbulb,
like a burrowing detective,
that only years of silence might answer,
without beating deadlines or running down clocks,
just aimless walks, slow food, and fruitful questioning.

Wandering the Country Planting Small Trees

The men in charge
of building the projects
of my childhood
decided, among themselves,
with their bulldozers, earth movers, and axes,
to dispatch every tree, all at once,
leaving no guardian behind
to cool the breeze,
or talk to,
or hide behind, or
lean against, for wondering.

So I found you where you live,
your rustling leaves waving hello
in the park,
on the lawn of the small-town library,
in the old Catholic cemetery,
and even in the Botanical Gardens among delicate
exotics,
you held me in your shadows.

Without the distractions of the everyday,
I think back to places where I've lived
and the lives I've left behind.

I wonder if the blue Palo Verde
still gossips with
the swarthy saguaro,
the prickly pear, the night blooming cereus,
and the miniature palm tree?

Does anyone whisper
how beautiful you are
to little gem magnolia
in the courtyard?
Do they stroke your thick, glossy leaves
the color of harmony and healing,
as your creamy petals fill the air
with honey perfume?

I still mourn the rustic assortment of conifers
that rested happily on loamy mounds
along the picket fence
in front of rolling commons
until that ill-fated summer
when the rains that never stopped
drowned you in your beds.

I could not live even a month
after replanting myself in the city of my youth
without you to attend to
in my tiny urban yard--
you with your papery platinum bark
and heart-shaped leaves that whirled
in the wind and broke the lonely silence.

Now I am here with two weepers
whose tendrils drape and dangle
like mother's arms over Boston Ivy
and ringlets of hostas,
the ornamental cherry waves at spring
with frivolous pink blossoms,
the red-headed maple
flirts with a sunbeam in the shade garden.

Watching

As the sepia sunrise lifts twilight's shade,
a zephyr swings by an old maple.
Flowers blush and sway
cooled by nature's crash and bluster.

Cardinals and blue jays sail from tree to fence to power
line
the envy of artists on the flying trapeze.
A red-bellied woodpecker
dressed for dinner in a scarlet turban and herringbone
suit,
slaked and sated, dons his tongue as a hat and flies
away.

The sun plays hide and seek with the clouds.
A butterscotch flower from the trumpet vine
who thought her life was over
pirouettes in the wind
and drops into a pool of water.

The neighbor's Russian Blue
darts across the yard
then stops mid-step and
stares through copper penny eyes
to assess my intentions.

Raindrops water the garden
and waltz in concentric circles
in the deep blue pool
then burst into a rabble of bubbles,
laughing.

Workshop

People show up by the dozen
to rake the dead leaves out of my poems
round them out with hedge trimmers
finish rough edges with pinking shears,
and leave them to bleed out in red ink.

Words tumble out
in ordered chaos—
subject, noun, verb,
a few articles, a dash of metaphor

full to bursting with sweet promise
to pour onto the page,
light or heavy, organic, homogenized, skimmed,
to be served at breakfast
in a bowl of rhyming couplets.

Worlds Crash

While the cat purrs on my lap
I tap the keys, letter by letter,

to make a sentence that becomes a stanza
about the autumn sun glowing on crimson leaves

the smell of musk wafting in the window
the low symphony of the music of water.

If you're not careful and take a wrong turn,
letters will screech to a halt

careen off the page
tumble end over end into the abyss

where there are no autumns, no symphonies,
where sunlight never falls

on the young man who weaponizes his computer
and takes pride in the kill count.

Sojourner Truth
(c. 1797-1883)

If women want rights more than they got, why don't
they just take them,
and not be talking about it.

When you were Isabella,
mother of five, after the torment of broken promises,
you walked away from the house of thrall,
infant Sophia in your arms,
into the unknown,
over the bristly footpaths
of the Hudson River Valley,
through pitch forests
where burning rods of tortures past
now merely limbs cluttered with leaves
brushing the starry sky.

Did the memory of your blind father,
starved and frozen on his pallet
in the hell of servitude
propel you on your journey?

Alone in the white world of lawyers and judges,
you cut a swath through thorny brambles
of race, gender, and class,
rescued your five-year-old son, Peter,
from the clutches of his Southern enslaver.

When Frances Gage
and the white assembly of women's rights
refused to let you speak

you took to the public square,
pushed the liberation boulder down
the steps of the Old Stone Church
declaring to the rapt crowd,
I am a woman's rights…as strong as any man
in a voice that swelled even the smallest heart,
in words that Abe Lincoln would remember you by

not the version that abolitionist Frances Gage turned
into *Ain't I a Woman*
as if you were a Southern slave who spoke minstrel.

The Narrative of Sojourner Truth 1850
The Anti-Slavery Bugle, Marius Robinson, June 21, 1851
New York Independent, Frances Gage, April 23, 1863
The Sojourner Truth Project

Marjory Stoneman Douglas
(1890-1998)

I knew nothing of you
until the boy invaded the school
bearing your name
with his assault rifle

and rained a hurricane of bullets
into 34 soft targets, leaving them
scattered like sunbathers
on a blood-soaked beach.

You knew what it was like,
with your breakdowns and lapses,
how the mind gets lost in the forest

but then you came along
with your clattering typewriter

and rescued the fragile Everglades
from madmen
intent on planting houses

where creatures with luminous eyes
slice through the shallows
carrying nothing but
musical scales on their backs
for Meadowlarks
to sing Mozart's *Requiem*

from choir lofts in the mangrove cathedral
with wings outstretched,
over the hallowed waters
you christened The River of Grass.

National Women's History Museum
Mariana Brandman, NWHM Predoctoral Fellow in Women's
History | 2020-2022

Marie-Thérèse Levasseur
(1721 – 1801)

--domestic partner of Jean-Jacques Rousseau

Bounty from the kind earth
bubbles in the pot on the stone hearth

when your water breaks
while you are writhing on the cold tile floor

Rousseau tears the infant
from your arms,
delivers him to a foundling home

then returns to the quiet
where he mines your shrewd intellect
to give birth to the Enlightenment

to pen the papers and books
on the origin of inequality, the social contract,
breastfeeding, the education of women,
and this advice on the raising of children:

**Take possession of him
as soon as he comes into the world
and keep him till he is a man.*

Each time your water breaks
where you kneel on the cold tile floor,
launder clothes in the wash basin,
empty the chamber pots,
sew buttons unraveled from a shirt

Rousseau tears the infants from your arms,
sends them to the foundling home

then amuses aristocratic women
with your malapropisms.

Marie Antoinette and her ladies at court
christen a charity in your name
for all the abandoned children
no one will pray for.

*Emile, Book I
The Wives of Western Philosophy – Forestal and Philips
7.) Therese Levasseur's Improvised Life with Rousseau
                         by Jennifer M. Jones
The Generalist Academy Rousseau's Children

Kitty Genovese
(1935-1964)

If nothing else it got us to think what we owe each other
 – Kitty's brother Bill

On the brief passage home
to Kew Gardens in Queens
in the sleepy darkness

Violence jabbed a blade
into her young body.

Neighbor Robert shouted from his window,
Let that girl alone!

Violence eclipsed into the shadows,
then, for the finale,
raped, robbed, and pierced her yet more
in the stairwell where she died
cradled in neighbor Sophia's arms.

While cries for help poured in,
Protect and Serve poured another coffee,
whiling away the hours on the graveyard shift
at the precinct.

To shield his squadron of do-nothings,
the *Chief of Protect and Serve*
told *Pulitzer Man* at *the journal of record*
a twisted tale of thirty-eight do-nothing neighbors

that exploded into a phenomenon
known as *bystander apathy*
to sell newspapers
to spark global outrage

and when confronted with the truth
to put right the lie,
Pulitzer Man said

it would ruin the story.

The Witness, documentary
 - William Genovese and James Solomon 2016

Beryl Markham

Did you marry three times
to cast yourself in traditional plays
when you were born to fly solo,
in the sky, on the earth,
in the bedrooms,
on the East African playground
you tell of, in mesmerizing prose?

While Kenyan women tended the nest,
there you were, even as a small girl,
spear in hand, invited to join in the hunt
with tribesmen, the men who later saved you
as you lay trapped and bleeding
under the claws of Mr. Elkington's lion.

As one of the first bush pilots,
you take us along on solo missions
into the pitch by light of moon
delivering supplies and people,
or desperately searching for a lost friend,
then relief and joy at the rescue.

Are you lost to the ages
because you are more than the child
who delivered Coquette's foal,
more than coaxing to gentle
even the most unwilling thoroughbreds,

more than the fiercest of free spirits,
the first to survive a solo, non-stop flight
over the Atlantic's fierce east to west winds?

I often take enchanted walks and thrilling rides
through the pages of *West with the Night,*
your memoir that plucked you from obscurity
and lifted you out of poverty in old age,
after someone excavated these words
among Hemingway's letters:

She writes so bloody wonderful,
so marvelously well…
she can write rings around all of us
who consider ourselves as writers.

Ode to the Water Gatherers

Blues drift from a neighbor's garage
as the garden hose dances,
snaps around my legs in kinks and tangles,
snags on a car tire
catches on a jagged rock.

A fairy waving a magic wand,
I quench the shading trees and cottage gardens

I think of you
in the frying pan heat of Sierra Leone
wrapped in a sarong slogging for miles
to ladle 40 pounds from the dirty water well
into a jerrican you carry on your crown
over a thick cloth halo;

I think of you
in your black burqa, in Yemen,
shackled waist to ankle with water jugs
that tear at your legs like talons
on the far journey to your village;

I think of you
so far from home
in monsoon-flooded Myanmar
your small bare feet slog through toxic mud
neck bent under buckets of foul water
that pitch and heave off the shoulder yoke.

Two boys bolt from behind on bicycles,
ride through the spray, legs splayed,
belt out whoops and squeals, turn around and do it
again,
cooling me in the mist.

Forgive me as I raise my eyes
to the snowball clouds that seem to deepen their blue
canvas
as the monarch drops by her milkweed patch
and I fill the bird bath to brimming.

About the Author

Donna Grace is a community activist, teacher and, with her husband George, co-host of the LitGarden Writers since 2008.

Prior to the pandemic, Donna rarely wrote poetry. At the onset of the pandemic, Donna discovered and took refuge in reading, studying, and writing poetry. Her earliest efforts were rewarded with two poems published in the Buffalo News Poetry Page; works included in LitGarden anthologies: *Just Twelve More Poems* and *Tilting Toward the Moon*; and featured readings at Circleformance; the Screening Room; Sea of Coffee in Canandaigua; Dog Ears 4th Friday Reading Series; The Buffalo Corner; Phil's Café at 40 Homer; Just Poets in Rochester; Literary Café @ Center For Inquiry; and Music and Poetry – A Musical Feast event at the Montante Cultural Center. Donna also enjoys listening to fellow poets and stepping up to the open mic at Cabernet Wine Café and Caffe Aroma.

Donna hopes you enjoy her first book, *Bread & Bisous*.

E-mail: donna4grace@gmail.com

Printed in the USA
CPSIA information can be obtained
at www.ICGtesting.com
CBHW052133060524
8165CB00030B/706